Trackers
0–3

by
Dr Hannah Mortimer

A QEd Publication

Published in 2003

© Hannah Mortimer

ISBN 1 898873 34 8

British Library Cataloguing
A catalogue record for this book is available from the British Library.

Published by QEd, The ROM Building, Eastern Avenue,
Lichfield, Staffs. WS13 6RN
Web site: www.qed.uk.com
Email: orders@qed.uk.com

Printed in the United Kingdom by Stowes (Stoke-on-Trent).

Contents

Page

Introduction 5
Who the Trackers are for 5
The four Aspects of Early Learning 5
Why track progress? 5
The Components 6
The Stepping Stones 7
How to use the Trackers 8
Planning the observations 9
Meeting individual needs 10
References 11

Aspects of Early Learning – A Strong Child 12
Me, Myself, I 13
Being Acknowledged and Affirmed 14
Developing Self-assurance 15
A Sense of Belonging 16

Aspects of Early Learning – A Skilful Communicator 17
Being Together 18
Finding a Voice 19
Listening and Responding 20
Making Meaning 21

Aspects of Early Learning – A Competent Learner 22
Making Connections – making sense 23
Making Connections – finding out 24
Making Connections – early maths 25
Being Imaginative 26
Being Creative – movement and touch 27
Being Creative – music 28
Being Creative – art and craft 29
Representing 30

Aspects of Early Learning – A Healthy Child   31
    Emotional Well-being   32
    Growing and Developing   33
    Keeping Safe   34
    Healthy Choices   35

Introduction

Who the Trackers are for

These progress trackers will be useful for early years educators working in all kinds of early years settings: pre-schools, private nurseries, day nurseries, Sure Start schemes and creches. It will also be helpful for individuals training on NVQ or pre-school diploma courses and of interest to childminders, parents and carers of children who are interested in tracking their children's development over the first three years.

The four Aspects of Early Learning

These Trackers have been designed to be simple and usable, yet to link into the Government's *Birth to three matters. A framework to support children in their earliest years* (Sure Start, 2003). The framework focuses on children and how they learn, rather than attempting to divide early learning into distinct skills and areas. Instead, it identifies four aspects of early learning:

- A Strong Child
- A Skilful Communicator
- A Competent Learner
- A Healthy Child

Each aspect is also divided into four Components, and these are reflected in the title page of each Tracker.

Why track progress?

The *National Standards for Full Day Care* (DfES, 2001a) state that the registered person should meet children's individual needs and promote their welfare. This will involve planning and providing activities and play opportunities to develop children's emotional, physical, social and intellectual capabilities (Standard 3). The registered person and staff are expected to observe and record what children do and use their observations to plan the next steps for the children's play, learning and development. Annex A adds that there should also be clear planning of babies' and toddlers' activities within the setting. You are also expected to be aware that some children may have special educational needs (SEN) and that you can take action to identify and meet these needs. You will be in a better position to do this if you have been able to observe and track the progress that any child is making.

While childcare workers have become familiar with the more traditional types of progress tracker based on child development stages (such as learning to stand or learning to talk) and skills learning (such as learning to feed oneself, learning to dress), it is more challenging for them to develop methods that are led by children's competencies. One of the first checklists to adopt this play-centred approach was the *Playladders* checklist (Mortimer, 2000) though these tend to start with the competencies of children of around 18 months old and do not correspond to the four Aspects. These present Trackers aim to serve as a bridge between the former methods and the new, providing confidence to workers that they can indeed track progress in a more holistic way. It is hoped that staff will use them flexibly and develop them further as they become more confident in moving away from a purely skills-led model. They should be used in conjunction with the framework of effective practice which explains in greater detail how to focus in on each Component.

The Components

Each page of the Trackers carries the title of one of the Components, yet weaves in some of the developmental and skills-based stages which users will already be familiar with and also builds in the Stepping Stones given in the Foundation Stage curriculum guidance.

A Strong Child

- Me, Myself and I (knowing who I am).
- Being Acknowledged and Affirmed (including friendships).
- Developing Self-assurance (including confidence).
- A Sense of Belonging (becoming a member of a social group).

A Skilful Communicator
- Being Together (communication).
- Finding a Voice (language expression).
- Listening and Responding (language reception).
- Making Meaning (both in comprehension and early literacy).

A Competent Learner
- Making Connections (making sense, finding out and early maths).
- Being Imaginative.
- Being Creative (movement and touch, music, art and craft).
- Representing (including early mark-making).

A Healthy Child
- Emotional Well-being (including self-help).
- Growing and Developing (including physical development and feeding).
- Keeping Safe.
- Healthy Choices (including personal hygiene).

Some Components have been given more than one page in order to include stages that users might be more familiar with.

The Stepping Stones
Nursery providers have asked for progress trackers to cover the first three years of life which overlap with the QCA Early Learning Goals and Stepping Stones for development. Though these progress trackers are divided into the four Aspects of *Birth to three matters* rather than the six Areas of Learning already familiar to those of you who work with children in the Foundation Stage of their early learning (age three to the end of the Reception year), there are footstep icons which tell you that certain of the statements relate closely to the Foundation Stage Stepping Stones. Because of this, you will be able

to carry forward information from the 0–3 Trackers to your records for three to five year-olds.

Each Tracker contains 16 areas of understanding or competence, most of which can be easily observed or easily interpreted using the Framework of effective practice. Some of these are taken from typical developmental stages that children pass through in their early years. Others relate to the Stepping Stones for early development given in the QCA/DfEE *Curriculum Guidance for the foundation stage* (2000). Stepping Stones are marked with this sign: *,* so that you can identify them easily. You will find it easier to decide whether what you are observing meets the Stepping Stones if you refer to the curriculum guidance document which has examples of children's play and learning behaviour at each of the stages. Sometimes the wording used in these progress trackers is slightly simplified from the actual Stepping Stones, but again referring to the full document will make sure your own assessment fits with the QCA/DfEE guidelines.

How to use the Trackers
Use one progress tracker booklet for each child. Observe the child during your daily play and care activities. If you feel that the child has reached that particular stage most of the time (we all have good days and bad days), then record the date of your observation in the column.

	✓	Date
Recognises parent or main carer		
Plays peep bo games		
Puts arms up to be lifted	✓	2/07/03
Pulls or tugs at adult to gain attention	✓	3/07/03

Revisit the Trackers at regular intervals. You will then find that you are gradually able to observe and record more and more skills as the child develops and gathers experiences.

Other settings prefer to adapt the recording column flexibly to suit their own recording system. For example, observations during each term are entered in a different colour with a single tick to indicate that the child sometimes manages that skill and double tick to indicate that the child has definitely mastered that skill and can demonstrate it in different situations. In other words, choose a system to suit your setting and keep it simple.

There is a space at the bottom for your additional comments if they are relevant. For example, you might wish to record that a child was poorly for a while in order to explain why there was a setback in their confidence. You might add a comment that a child went into hospital for grommets on a certain date and that might explain why speech and understanding suddenly improved. You might want to use the Trackers more flexibly and add qualifying comments such as 'only if his familiar helper is there'.

Make sure that you have actual evidence for each of the items you record. Work on your actual observations rather than on hearsay. This is simply because you need to know which items still need encouragement or teaching and which are well established as part of the child's repertoire.

Planning the observations
Some settings find it easiest to delegate responsibility for the tracking to different members of staff. For example, each child could be assigned to one key worker who would be responsible for tracking the development of a small group of children. Other settings might ascribe a certain Aspect to a particular member of staff who would also have the responsibility for planning and developing opportunities and activities in that area for that term.

Plan certain activities or opportunities that are going to allow you to observe a particular aspect of all the children's development that session, for example sand play.

Make all observations in as natural a way as possible so that the children are not aware of a different situation or the fact that you are assessing them.

Build in regular opportunities for observing as part of your regular short-term, medium-term and long-term planning.

Find regular opportunities to share progress with parents and carers. Compare notes and share successes.

Meeting individual needs
As part of your regular observing, you may notice that a particular child is developing rather patchily. Perhaps there is one or more aspect of their development that is not progressing as fast as the others. This provides you with useful information for planning new learning opportunities for that child. Because the progress trackers make you aware of the possible next steps that each child passes through, you can play alongside the child to teach and encourage that step. The Trackers are not set out rigorously in developmental sequence and each child will develop individually. However, there is an approximate progression from nought to three with the youngest stages at the top of each page to the oldest stage at the bottom.

Sometimes you might be aware that a child has special educational needs because his/her development is significantly behind what you would normally expect for that age. You can still use your Trackers to plan for next steps. You might also find the *Playladders* checklist (also from QEd Publications) a useful tool for observing and supporting children with SEN in your setting. You will also need to refer to *The Special Educational Needs Code of Practice* (DfES, 2001b), or refer to the Early Years booklet on this topic published by QEd Publications.

A *Trackers* booklet has also been produced for the three to five year-old group by QEd Publications.

References

DfES (2001a) *National Standards for Full Day Care*. Nottingham: DfES Publications.

DfES (2001b) *The Special Educational Needs Code of Practice*. Nottingham: DfES Publications.

Mortimer, H. (2000) *Playladders*. Lichfield: QEd Publications.

Mortimer, H. (2002) *The SEN Code of Practice in Early Years Settings*. Lichfield: QEd Publications.

Qualifications and Curriculum Authority (QCA) (2000) *Curriculum Guidance for the foundation stage*. Hayes: QCA Publications.

Sure Start (2003) *Birth to three matters. A framework to support children in their earliest years*. Nottingham: DfES Publications.

Aspects of Early Learning

A Strong Child

- Me, Myself, I
- Being Acknowledged and Affirmed
- Developing Self-assurance
- A Sense of Belonging

Trackers   0–3

Aspect of learning	A Strong Child
Component	Me, Myself, I

	✓	Date
Alert and interested between sleeps		
Coos and gurgles when happy		
Plays with own fists and feet		
Turns when you call their name		
Waves bye bye		
Smiles at own reflection and pats mirror		
Expresses feelings about a significant personal event 👣		
Tells you their name		
Can tell you if they are a boy or a girl		
Begins to differentiate between past and present 👣		
Shows an interest in photographs of their lives 👣		
Adapts behaviour to different occasions 👣		
Engages in imaginative play based on their own experiences 👣		
Makes connections between their life experiences 👣		
Shows care and concern for self 👣		
Shows strong sense of self 👣		

Comments

Trackers   0–3

Aspect of learning	A Strong Child
Component	Being Acknowledged and Affirmed

	✓	Date
Recognises parent or main carer		
Plays peep bo games		
Puts arms up to be lifted		
Pulls or tugs at adult to gain attention		
Joins in an organised play activity for five minutes		
Seeks out others to share experiences 👣		
Relates and makes attachments to adults in the group 👣		
Joins in an organised play activity for ten minutes		
Greets people appropriately		
Relates and makes attachments to other children 👣		
Can share toys with adult support		
Can tell you who their friends are		
Enjoys playing cooperatively with other children		
Can share a toy with another child		
Recognises when others are happy/sad/angry		
Can take turns		

Comments

Trackers   0–3

Aspect of learning	A Strong Child
Component	Developing Self-assurance

	✓	Date
Can be settled for a sleep		
Is comforted by close body contact		
Passes a toy to you on request		
Separates from main carer with support 👣		
Accepts presence of another child close by		
Chooses what toy to play with next 👣		
Shows curiosity 👣		
Shows a sense of pride in own achievement 👣		
Shows an awareness of change 👣		
Trusts an adult with a favourite toy 👣		
Loves to explore the playroom 👣		
Enjoys new experiences 👣		
Can show another child what to do		
Will join in a large group		
Chooses own activity to do next 👣		
Separates from main carer with confidence 👣		

Comments

Trackers   0–3

Aspect of learning	A Strong Child
Component	A Sense of Belonging

	✓	Date
Snuggles in when held		
Appears to feel safe and secure in the group 👣		
Watches a moving person		
Is wary of strangers		
Enjoys being with other children		
Likes to have a familiar adult nearby		
Watches other children playing		
Plays alongside another child with an adult joining in		
Enjoys playing in parallel to other children		
Talks about who their friends are		
Plays with a group of children in the home corner		
Helps actively at tidy up time		
Knows the names of several other children		
Shows care and concern for others 👣		
Shows an interest in the world in which they live 👣		
Has a sense of belonging to the group 👣		

Comments

Aspects of Early Learning

A Skilful Communicator

- Being Together
- Finding a Voice
- Listening and Responding
- Making Meaning

Trackers   0–3

Aspect of learning	A Skilful Communicator
Component	Being Together

	✓	Date
Cries when distressed		
Turns eyes towards person talking		
Shouts to attract attention		
Laughs and chuckles		
Shows pleasure when cuddled and tickled		
Turns to you when you call		
Watches speaker during a conversation		
Settles with an adult to share a short picture book		
Passes a toy to a named person		
Selects and shares a picture book with an adult		
Pretends to read a story to someone else		
Joins in a simple action rhyme		
Interrupts a story with their own ideas		
Joins in action rhymes in a group		
Talks easily to familiar adults		
Talks easily to other children		

Comments

Trackers   0–3

Aspect of learning	A Skilful Communicator
Component	Finding a Voice

	✓	Date
Cries differently due to different discomforts		
Makes sounds when an adult speaks to them		
Makes a range of speech sounds		
Babbles in long strings (e.g. 'ma – ma – ma')		
Says one or two words with meaning		
Asks for toys with sounds as well as gestures 👣		
Says no purposefully		
Uses six or more recognisable words		
Puts two words together		
Uses 50 or more recognisable words 👣		
Speaks in short phrases 👣		
Uses tone and rhythm to add meaning 👣		
Uses me/you 👣		
Asks questions 👣		
Holds a simple conversation		
Remembers and talks about things that have happened to them 👣		

Comments

Trackers   0–3

Aspect of learning	A Skilful Communicator
Component	Listening and Responding

	✓	Date
Startled by sudden, loud noises		
Turns head towards a voice		
Responds to the sound of crinkly paper		
Turns head towards a hidden sound		
Echoes a sound (e.g. 'ba – ba')		
Distinguishes one sound from another 👣		
Responds to bye bye		
Listens to favourite nursery rhymes 👣		
Listens to other children talking 👣		
Listens to instructions one-to-one		
Listens to short stories 👣		
Listens to instructions in a small group		
Listens to and repeats a three-word phrase		
Enjoys rhyming games 👣		
Tells you why a story was enjoyed		
Enjoys an increasing range of books 👣		

Comments

Trackers 0–3

Aspect of learning	A Skilful Communicator
Component	Making Meaning

	✓	Date
Looks briefly at pictures – one object per page		
Looks at pictures as adult turns pages		
Anticipates what happens next in a familiar rhyme		
Gives you a named object		
Points to four body parts when named		
Follows familiar instructions (e.g. clap hands)		
Points to a named picture		
Answers yes/no questions		
Responds to simple directions		
Has favourite books		
Asks what? and why? questions		
Handles books carefully		
Suggests how a story might end		
Holds book correctly and turns pages		
Follows a two-part instruction (e.g. this then that)		
Answers simple questions		

Comments

Aspects of Early Learning

A Competent Learner

- Making Connections – making sense
- Making Connections – finding out
- Making Connections – early maths
- Being Imaginative
- Being Creative – movement and touch
- Being Creative – music
- Being Creative – art and craft
- Representing

Trackers   0–3

Aspect of learning	A Competent Learner
Component	Making Connections – making sense

	✓	Date
Stops fretting as adult approaches		
Explores objects using mouthing and touch		
Looks for fallen toy		
Links cause with effect (e.g. with pop-up toy)		
Matches red/blue cup to red/blue saucer		
Matches shoes and socks		
Explores objects using wide range of play		
Sorts the farm animals into sets		
Shows repeated patterns of play (e.g. putting one thing inside the other)		
Talks about what is happening		
Shows an interest in why things happen		
Sorts objects by one function		
Assembles a train track or road layout		
Describes simple features of objects and events		
Builds a simple bridge		
Talks about tomorrow or yesterday		

Comments

Trackers   0–3

Aspect of learning	A Competent Learner
Component	Making Connections – finding out

	✓	Date
Enjoys handling small toys		
Unwraps a hidden toy or present		
Shows an interest in new toys		
Anticipates an action in a familiar rhyme		
Plays with a simple shape posting toy		
Stacks bricks to make a tower		
Opens boxes or containers to explore		
Explores which things roll		
Can complete simple inset puzzles 👣		
Explores which things sink or float		
Shows an interest in new activities		
Can fit stacking beakers on top of each other		
Completes a simple six-piece jigsaw		
Shows an interest in how things work 👣		
Shows an interest in computers (ICT) 👣		
Shows evidence of forward planning		

Comments

Trackers   0–3

Aspect of learning	A Competent Learner
Component	Making Connections – early maths

	✓	Date
Handles and explores shapes		
Fills and empties containers		
Can give you the big one		
Shows an interest when you count steps		
Uses some number names spontaneously		
Matches cups to saucers, one-to-one		
Finds another shape the same		
Joins in number rhymes and songs		
Makes arrangements with shapes or small toys		
Exchanges money in nursery shop		
Notices round or square shapes around the room		
Uses number language in play		
Uses words like in, on and under		
Uses words like big and little		
Selects best shape to fit a space		
Compares two groups of objects saying when they have the same number		

Comments

Trackers   0–3

Aspect of learning	A Competent Learner
Component	Being Imaginative

	✓	Date
Copies facial expressions (e.g. looks serious when adult does)		
Copies raising both hands in the air		
Imitates hand clapping		
Cuddles a teddy or doll		
Rolls a car along making noises		
Copies adult doing routine things		
Puts doll into bed or buggy		
Makes a pretend cup of tea		
Plays on own in home corner		
Adapts home corner to suit a new game		
Uses different tones of voice in imaginary play		
Enjoys dressing up		
Finds own props to support their play		
Acts out a familiar story with help		
Pretends to be someone else		
Develops an imaginative game with their own ideas		

Comments

Trackers   0–3

Aspect of learning	A Competent Learner
Component	Being Creative – movement and touch

	✓	Date
Uses body to explore texture and space		
Watches movement of own hand in front of face		
Crawls towards a colourful ball		
Enjoys splashing with water		
Enjoys manipulating sand		
Uses single finger to point or poke		
Buries and finds toys in the sand		
Shows an interest in what they touch and feel		
Shows curiosity, observes and manipulates objects		
Moulds wet sand		
Kicks and rolls a large ball		
Rolls a ball to knock down a skittle		
Begins to describe the texture of things		
Operates equipment using pushing and pulling movements		
Uses one-handed tools and equipment		
Joins in a simple ball game		

Comments

Trackers   0–3

Aspect of learning	A Competent Learner
Component	Being Creative – music

	✓	Date
Stops fretting when soft music is played		
Enjoys a one-two rocking rhythm		
Shows curiosity and interest by facial expression, movement or sound		
Explores objects by banging		
Kicks and waves arms to music		
Shows an interest in what they hear		
Looks at you when you sing		
Makes noises to music		
Shakes a rattle		
Shows an interest in the way musical instruments sound		
Pats a drum or tambourine		
Joins a simple action rhyme		
Responds to sound with body movements		
Recognises familiar songs		
Joins in with dancing and singing games		
Joins in with favourite songs		

Comments

Trackers 0–3

Aspect of learning	A Competent Learner
Component	Being Creative – art and craft

	✓	Date
Enjoys watching colours or lights		
Enjoys crumpling and tearing paper		
Enjoys handling collage material		
Dabs with a glue stick		
Sticks one craft piece to another		
Shows an interest in what they see 👣		
Manipulates play dough		
Makes patterns in the sand		
Uses tools to model dough		
Begins to differentiate colours 👣		
Enjoys painting using several colours		
Snips with scissors		
Makes three-dimensional structures 👣		
Chooses best materials for own model 👣		
Makes simple models/patterns with construction toy 👣		
Makes simple models from scrap materials 👣		

Comments

Trackers   0–3

Aspect of learning	A Competent Learner
Component	Representing

	✓	Date
Makes musical noises		
Makes paint marks on paper *✔*		
Holds a chubby pencil between thumb and first two fingers		
Pretends that one object represents another *✔*		
Makes faint strokes and dabs with pencil		
Scribbles boldly		
Scribbles round and round		
Uses lines to enclose a space with dots and dabs inside *✔*		
Pretends to write		
Draws a person		
Copies O and +		
Dances to music		
Understands that a printed word means something *✔*		
Forms several letter shapes		
Reads one or two numbers		
Writes part of own name		

Comments

Aspects of Early Learning

A Healthy Child

- Emotional Well-being
- Growing and Developing
- Keeping Safe
- Healthy Choices

Trackers 0–3

Aspect of learning	A Healthy Child
Component	Emotional Well-being

	✓	Date
Smiles back at adult		
Looks towards a familiar carer when upset		
Lets adult know when cross/upset/happy by behaving differently		
Moves arms and legs helpfully when being changed		
Pulls off loose socks		
Undresses with help		
Seeks comfort when upset		
Stays within play area		
Puts on own slippers or boots (sometimes wrong feet)		
Can tell you if sad/cross/happy		
Shows willingness to tackle problems		
Enjoys self-chosen challenges		
Puts on own coat if helped with fastenings		
Familiar with the daily routine		
Manages large buttons		
Dresses independently		

Comments

Trackers   0–3

Aspect of learning	A Healthy Child
Component	Growing and Developing

	✓	Date
Raises arms to bottle		
Crawls over rugs and cushions		
Sits independently		
Drinks from baby cup held by adult		
Rejects unwanted bottle, cup or spoon		
Feeds self with fingers		
Walks independently		
Crawls through a short tunnel		
Drinks independently from a cup with a spout		
Eats food (messily) with a spoon		
Trots quickly		
Drinks independently from an open cup		
Eats with spoon and fork		
Uses a knife and fork when food is cut up		
Runs quickly		
Peddles a toddler bike or car		

Comments

Trackers   0–3

Aspect of learning	A Healthy Child
Component	Keeping Safe

	✓	Date
Pulls light cover off face		
Can be distracted from doing something		
Stands steadily without falling		
Steps around or over an obstacle		
Finds a space to sit down in		
Accepts no without too much fuss		
Understands how to be gentle		
Seeks help when it is needed		
Reaches high on tiptoes without falling		
Avoids collisions when on wheeled toys		
Does what is nicely asked 50% of the time		
Can stop on request		
Avoids obstacles when moving fast		
Climbs safely on low climbing frame		
Avoids dangers when playing		
Negotiates a toddler slide		

Comments

Trackers   0–3

Aspect of learning	A Healthy Child
Component	Healthy Choices

	✓	Date
Accepts having nappy changed		
Turns face away when refusing food		
Tugs at wet or dirty nappy		
Helps to wash and dry own hands		
Indicates a choice by pointing		
Has successes in the potty		
Indicates when toilet needed with some accidents		
Can indicate choice by using yes/no		
Indicates wish for a drink when thirsty		
Bowel control during the day		
Makes choices at mealtimes		
Able to go to toilet alone		
Selects warm clothes when it is cold		
Begins to accept the needs of others with support		
Takes initiatives in organising self 👣		
Begins to understand the need to stay healthy and clean 👣		

Comments